CATHOLIC
& NEWLY MARRIED

5 CHALLENGES AND 5 OPPORTUNITIES

Kathy and Steve Beirne

acta
PUBLICATIONS

CATHOLIC & NEWLY MARRIED
5 CHALLENGES AND 5 OPPORTUNITIES
by Kathy and Steve Beirne

Edited by Gregory F. Augustine Pierce
Cover and text design and typesetting by Patricia A. Lynch
Cover photo Sadik Demiroz, Bigstock
Illustrations: Kari Lehr, Birch Design Studio

Scripture taken from *The Message.* Copyright © 1993, 1994, 1995, 1996, 2000, 2001, 2002. Used by permission of NavPress Publishing Group.

Published by ACTA Publications, 4848 N. Clark Street, Chicago, IL 60640, (800) 397-2282, www.actapublications.com

Library of Congress Catalogue Number: 2012940549
ISBN: 978-0-87946-493-6
Printed in the United States of America by Total Printing Systems
Year 25 24 23 22 21 20 19 18 17 16 15
Printing 20 19 18 17 16 15 14 13 12 11 10 9 8 7 6 5 4 3 2

♻ Text printed on 30% post-consumer recycled paper

CONTENTS

DEDICATION

To the marriage preparation team we have worked with in Portland, Maine, for your dedication, inspiration, humor and esprit de corps. You embody what being Catholic and being married mean in the most believable and approachable ways.

INTRODUCTION

Here is what we have learned from our marriage and those of the many others we have had the privilege to observe, support, guide, bless, and celebrate.

Our first years of marriage remain in our minds like a merging of two streams coming down to form a river—a lot of turbulence while the waters intermingled. We entered with two very different sets of skills and expectations. Kathy came from a family that put a lot of emphasis on competition. Her family played cards and board games, argued at the table about sports and politics and religion, and assumed they would compete in school for good grades. Steve's family strove for different goals. They were expected to be polite to one another, to know all the finer points of etiquette, to be genial, quick witted, and hard working.

While these two family systems weren't mutually exclusive, they did create some interesting (and some painful) things for us to negotiate.

When Kathy would argue a point, Steve would back off but be offended by her tone of voice. When we would have a difference in our relationship, Steve would assume if he didn't pursue the topic it was over, while Kathy felt that there should be some agreed-upon settlement or conclusion. Kathy expected Steve to be interested in, and up on, political topics. And Steve actually expected Kathy to know which fork to use at formal dinners!

These many years later, some of the things that went on then make us laugh and some make us cringe. But the bottom line is that we worked through them to have the caring, happy, egalitarian marriage that we wake up to each day. That doesn't mean we don't still have differences, but we know how to negotiate those differences. As Steve said recently, the risk to each of us is much less. We are "happily married," which we're sure is your goal as well. Each of us believes it would take a volcano to disrupt what we have spent a lifetime building.

We also have spent a good part of our lives helping other couples work to build solid foundations for their marriages. We see ourselves as cheerleaders, urging couples to keep working at loving each other, understanding each other, forgiving each other, and forging the lifelong friendship every couple we ever knew was looking for when they got married.

For us, our Catholic faith has been a major part of the fabric of our marriage. Each of us was raised in a Catholic home and attended Catholic schools, but once again we discovered our faith was different in ways that might have looked on the surface to be the same. Kathy's home was one that encouraged discussion of questions about faith and doctrine. They had many books and magazines available. They were familiar with major Catholic authors. Steve's family had a more devotional approach to their Catholic faith. He grew up saying the rosary, attending parish devotions like Adoration of the Blessed Sacrament and the Stations of the Cross, and had many religious statues in his home.

Despite different styles or approaches to our shared religious tradition, however, we both see the world through the lens of our faith, and this has a profound effect on all our marital decisions, from how to raise our kids to where to go on vacation. Catholicism is for us now an adult faith that challenges and inspires us to work to deepen and strengthen our relationship and to contribute in a meaningful way to making our world a better place, a little more like the Kingdom of God that Jesus envisioned for all people, including our children and our children's children.

An important fact we have come to realize as we have worked with different couples is that *every* "Catholic" marriage is an "interfaith marriage" in religious terms, no matter

Seeing the world through the lens of faith has a profound effect on all our marital decisions, from how to raise our kids to where to go on vacation.

whether it is between two Catholics, a Catholic and a Christian of another denomination, a Catholic and a non-Christian believer of another faith, or a Catholic and a person of no professed religion. Each person in a marriage has, almost by definition, different religious experiences, backgrounds, views, and practices when they enter marriage. One of the sets of challenges *and* opportunities we present here is to learn to respect those differences, seek common ground where possible, and practice mutual respect always.

There are a limitless number of challenges and opportunities that face a couple when they start a marriage, and there are all kinds of marriages that result from the choices a couple makes from the options presented to them. This little book outlines five challenges and five opportunities we know you will have as you start to build your own marriage. We would like to be *your* cheerleaders, encouraging you to do the hard but fulfilling work of building a great marriage.

May God bless you both.
Kathy and Steve Beirne
Portland, Maine

FIRST CHALLENGE

Learning to speak the same language is a lot harder than it seems.

Just because you're new to marriage doesn't mean you're new to your relationship. You may have been together for several years before you tied the knot. But making the public commitment that is the heart of marriage can sometimes change the way you communicate with one another. There's something about that "til death do us part" that creates a different tone to discussions.

For example, it may be you find yourself acting more like your mother or father in conversations now that you're married. Patterns that you grew up hearing have a powerful effect on you, and may emerge now that you are in similar roles to those of your parents. Many people have this experience. Old "tapes" in their heads spring up and they say things they heard at home a million times in their childhood, even when they swore "I'll never be like that."

Sometimes making the decision to marry has been concurrent with other changes in your life. You've decided to buy a house, for example, or decided to start a family. So new stresses or new expectations have changed the game.

Maybe you have recently become aware of a certain kind of body language from your partner that speaks to you of resistance to your ideas. Maybe he or she turns away as you talk, or rolls his or her eyes. Body language can be a hard thing to deal with, because it's largely an interpretation and

Learn to tell the other person what you are "hearing" them say, even if it is non-verbally.

therefore easily denied: "I did not smirk!" or "I shrugged my shoulders because I didn't care, not because I disagreed." We all do this, and often unconsciously, but it does interfere with a couple's effort to talk honestly and openly and effectively with each other. Learn to tell the other person what you are "hearing" him or her say, even if it is non-verbally.

You may already be aware that one of you is more of an introvert and one more of an extrovert. That means one of you needs time to process information while the other needs to talk out an idea in order to know how you feel about something. We know several couples who have felt the frustration of having these different ways of processing information and making decisions. There is no one right way to handle this personality difference, but it is very important to understand and honor the preferences of your spouse in how to deal with things.

Gender differences, too, may become more apparent after you are married for a while. Traditionally women are much more comfortable with conversations about feelings

—studies show they even have a much larger vocabulary of feeling words! So it is not uncommon for a man to feel disadvantaged in a dialogue that involves how each person is feeling. Men on the other hand, assume their wife knows how they feel and are often surprised to find she does not. While you were dating it may have been easier to walk away from these differences in communication styles, but now there may be less psychic space within which to maneuver.

So how do you face the challenges of learning to speak the same language? Here are some suggestions.

■ Ask yourself what you hope to get out of a particular discussion. Do you hope to win? Do you want to avoid a disagreement or, at the least, avoid blame? Do you just want to get it over with and return to what you were doing? Or do you want to discuss an issue, resolve it one way or the other, either by compromise or by one side or the other "giving in." (By the way, "giving in" is not a bad thing, especially on unimportant issues. In fact, we believe both sides in a marriage should feel that their partner gives in more than half the time—that is, neither "wins" all the time and that their spouse is the more generous one.)

■ "Peace at any price" makes for a quieter household, but not necessarily a more harmonious one. Some issues are not meant for "giving in," they need to be talked through, thought about, talked through again. Sometimes you will get emotional, even angry. Still, a decision has to be made that both husband and wife can live with, sometimes for the rest of their marriage (such as questions about having and raising children). Couples are not always at their best in these uncomfortable conversations. Trying to keep a goal in mind helps to tailor a disagreement in a specific direction. The fact is that there are always problems that need to be talked out and solved for the good of a marriage, but it's important not to make them a contest that one side wins and the other side loses.

■ One specific suggestion we have is to consider learning about the Meyers Briggs Temperament Inventory. It's a tool that may allow you to understand each other's preferences for taking in and sharing information. A couple we know said that knowing each other's personality strengths allowed them to divide up responsibilities in their decision-making. She is better at gathering information, for example, and he is better about making decisions based on that input. This knowledge of how they both operate has made for a smoother path in their marriage.

■ "Watch the way you talk. Let nothing foul or dirty come out of your mouth. Say only what helps, each word a gift" (Ephesians 4:29). Check out the Scriptures for places where they speak about having a respectful, loving, reciprocal style. All conversations are essentially spiritual in nature, because they engage the spirit, not just the mind. Some couples have a more volatile style and often have more "spirited" disagreements. That's okay, as long as you don't cross a line and say things you can't take back easily.

■ Here are some Rules for Fighting Fair:

> We will find a time to talk when there is any difficulty or hard feelings.

> If we are angry, we'll make that time only after we have cooled down.

> We agree never to strike out at one another, either by calling names or using physical force.

> We will treat all eruptions of anger as something that needs to be solved by the two of us for the sake of our marriage.

> We will not use the words "always" or "never" when disagreeing.

> We will not bring up past behaviors or blame our families of origin or try to get our children on our side against the other.

> We will not use the silent treatment, make accusations, attempt to talk over our partner, or embarrass each other in front of our children or others.

 **All conversations are essentially spiritual in nature, because they engage the spirit, not just the mind.**

› We will not talk behind each other's backs to our friends or families.

› If we can't solve a problem ourselves, we agree to seek professional help (counselor, minister, life coach, mediator) sooner rather than later.

■ Learn to reframe things that bother you. A wife was annoyed that her husband would always leave a residue of food in the sink when he did the dishes. After complaining to no avail, she began to think, "I have a husband who does the dishes and all I have to do is empty out that little drain." A husband was upset because his wife liked to channel surf when they were watching television, but then he realized that she often found a better show for both of them by doing so. Looking at an irritant from a different perspective sometimes changes your feelings about it.

■ Be clear about things that bother you, but try to do it in a thoughtful way: "I appreciate that fact that you're such a hard worker and need to relax when you get home, but is there any way we could talk about something that is bothering me?" If your spouse says that it is not a good time, take it at face value and ask if you might discuss it the next day or whenever seems like a good time. Then remember to do so: "Remember that you said it would be okay if I brought up something that is bothering me?" And don't forget the power of touch—an arm around a shoulder or taking your partner's hand can be a nice way to ease into a conversation.

FIRST OPPORTUNITY

Improving your communications skills in marriage will help with the rest of your life as well.

No matter where you are on the communications scale—from poor to excellent—there is always an opportunity to improve. Marriage offers a chance to work on those skills in what should be a safe and loving relationship. Or to put it another way, if you can't communicate with your wife (or husband), who can you communicate with?

Being married is an "all in" experience. Strengthening your communication skills will strengthen your marriage, and the commitment you both make to learning how to communicate well with each other will pay dividends not only in your marriage but in other aspects of your lives, including your work; childrearing; dealing with friends, family, and in-laws; as well as in your community and civic activities.

Consider how you might improve the ways you communicate with your spouse. Speaking and listening skills are no different than other skills you wish to acquire or perfect. There are countless resources available to married couples to help them improve their communication. Any bookseller will have entire sections devoted to the topic. Almost all marriage preparation or enrichment courses offered by churches and dioceses contain information about skills and techniques that have proven helpful for other couples. Most of these programs are research-based and have been tested with many couples.

The beauty of marriage is that if one person changes his or her behavior the other person has to notice.

The internet also offers lots of help. If you search under "communications skills for married couples" over two million references will show up! Start with the first ten links and see if anything interests you. This search can be done as a couple or, if you can't budge your husband or wife from the TV set, start by doing the research yourself. The beauty of marriage is that if one person changes his or her behavior the other person has to notice.

There is a story about one young wife who complained that her husband never thanked her for all she did for him. As much and as often as she pointed out this lack of appreciation to him, however, his behavior never changed. Whatever communication-improvement source she was using advised her to stop complaining and to start showing appreciation for whatever things, however small, her husband did around the house, so she did. "Honey, thanks for putting the dishes away." "I appreciate your stopping at the store for the milk and bread." "I notice how nice you were to my mother when she was over to the house yesterday."

These were insignificant things her husband was doing, hardly worthy of note at all. But in just a few weeks he began to compliment her in a similar manner, telling her what a good cook she was and thanking her for picking up the clothes in the bathroom. He even brought her a small present for no reason, something he had never done before.

The point is that his behavior changed because she changed her strategy. Instead of complaining, she praised. Instead of being resentful, she looked for ways to be positive.

"That's not fair" you might say. "Why should she have to do all the work? He's the one in the wrong."

Our response is that what she was doing wasn't working and that the new strategy got her what she wanted: a new level of communication with her husband. It was a simple technique every counselor knows, but her changed behavior brought about her desired outcome.

We also want to suggest that perhaps the young husband might not have had the family background or life experiences that taught him how to show his love and appreciation the way his wife could see and hear it. So the wife simply demonstrated the behavior she was looking for, and the husband responded in kind. That's why some people say that couples begin to act like (and sometime even look like) each other after they have been married for many years. What is really happening is that couples learn behavior from each other that then becomes how they relate to each other, their children, and others outside the marriage itself.

Observe other couples whose marriages you truly admire. How do they talk to each other? How do they listen?

Imitate what you observe. Don't worry that it seems awkward at first. Like any new behavior, better communication between you and your spouse will get easier over time.

Here are some basic rules for good communication between a husband and a wife.

Whenever you communicate, do so:

> › With real kindness and respect.
> › With genuine interest and attention.
> › With unfailing courtesy and love.
> › With abundant affirmation and praise.
> › With mutual gratitude and appreciation.
> › With the best interests of your relationship always at heart.

It's amazing that at times we don't give the person we love more than anyone else in the world—our beloved spouse—the same regard we automatically give a stranger or guest in our home. It's not that we don't love the person we betrothed. Sometimes we simply take our marital love for granted and assume our spouse knows we love him or her. But the opportunity we have in marriage is to learn to let others know how much we love them in verbal and nonverbal ways. Why? Because it builds good will and strengthens the bond between people—and that is one thing this tired world can never get too much of!

SECOND CHALLENGE

Getting along with in-laws can be stressful and takes time, energy, and sometimes creativity.

Life is full of unintended consequences. You fall in love with an amazing person and suddenly realize that embracing that person means embracing a whole lot of other people with their own set of customs, behaviors, and beliefs, many of whom have a much longer relationship with your spouse than you do...not to mention that pesky genetic component. That is why we call them our "families of origin."

Customs can include anything from what meats can be served at the annual 4th of July barbecue to the obligatory Christmas Eve dinner with eight kinds of fish. We had a friend who married a Turkish man whose mother-in-law wanted her to embed a blue bead in their first child's forehead to ward off evil spirits. Most married couples don't have to face anything that dramatic, but family customs around holidays, birthdays, anniversaries, and especially the raising of children are all things that might make you uncomfortable.

Behaviors can also be a challenge. At a marriage prep class recently, a young woman told how her family loved to gather for coffee and argue over politics. They held very different points of view and didn't mind expressing them loudly. She was delighted to be entering a family where that was not the way political differences were handled, and she was embarrassed to expose her fiancé to what went on in her family. It turned out, however, that eventually it bothered her that no one in her husband's family ever expressed a political opinion and that when she did so the conversation was always changed immediately!

How families of origin express affection can also sometimes create tension. A friend of ours who came from a very reserved family married into his wife's family, where everyone hugs and kisses at every opportunity. He actually found that he would try to position himself behind chairs when his mother-in-law was around so he didn't have to embrace her over and over again. The man has learned to accept the more demonstrative behaviors of his wife's family, but the constant show of affection still feels a little foreign to him.

Faith practices also differ widely in couples, even when both were raised Catholic. And if the two of you don't come from the same Christian tradition, then your in-laws may have inaccurate ideas about your denomination. Baptists, for example, may want to know what the Vatican does with all its money. Catholics may wonder if Mormon baptism really "counts." And if your in-laws are Muslim or Jewish or Buddhist or Hindu or even agnostic or atheist, you and your spouse are both going to have a lot of communicating to do—with your in-laws and with each other and, presumably, between the two sets of in-laws themselves.

In our current society, you also may have more than one set of in-laws to deal with. Mother and stepfather, father and stepmother often don't get along well with each other, and you have to figure out how to get along with both. Or if one set of parents is divorced and one or both have not remarried,

Family is family, and your job is to try to get along with your spouse's, almost more than your own!

you might have some real juggling to do around family events.

There are also questions about relatives' sexual orientation, political views, religious affiliation, or economic situation that have to be negotiated. Your loyalty to your spouse will definitely color the way you react to and interact with the cast of characters. If your spouse does not have a good relationship with his or her stepmother, for example, it will be hard for you to see the woman objectively. But still you must try, even if your spouse doesn't seem to or care whether you do or not. Family is family, and your job is to try to get along with your spouse's, almost more than your own!

Each of the different aspects of life with families of origin provide a spiderweb of challenges, but couples have been dealing with them for as long as there have been marriages, so here are a few time-tested ways of handling the potential tensions.

Let your spouse take the lead when dealing with his or her family.

■ Let your spouse take the lead when dealing with his or her family. If your brother-in-law insults you at the family picnic, let your husband or wife call him up and do the ironing out. If your mom made a remark about your spouse's grooming or financial acumen, you be the one to smooth the path. It's usually best to leave the negotiating, apologizing, and confronting in the capable hands of someone who has lived with these people for a lifetime.

■ If there is something going on that neither of you likes (like relatives who want to argue over politics) then the two of you can decide together how you want to handle it. You might just stay away from those sessions, or get up from the table and walk away when the exchanges get heated. You are a family unit yourselves now, and you have the right to establish your own rules. You don't have to be "in your face" about it, but it helps to realize that the two of you have a private agreement on how to handle a particular situation that comes up regularly.

■ Work to see the good in your spouse's family. After all, they produced the person you love, so there must be something about them that is admirable. Likewise, don't feel you have to defend you own family no matter what they do. You are an adult now, and you can love your family of origin and still recognize how they might drive your spouse crazy sometimes.

■ Sometimes you might feel like your spouse's family of origin is more important to him or her than you are. Take a step back before raising something like that, because it could put your husband or wife into a position of feeling that he or she has to choose between you and his or her family. Even if you win that choice, you might lose something important. After all, it's really not a competition, even if it is just one of you and all of them. If you don't force a choice, your role as spouse should ultimately be secure.

Remember: Who your in-laws are is not something you have any choice about. How you respond to them, however, is directly within your control.

SECOND OPPORTUNITY

Learning to see your in-laws as resources can be marriage-enriching.

Have you ever come into a play or movie after it had already started? It can be confusing at best and irritating at worst. Sometimes you want to just start all over. That's what it might feel like when you begin the process of joining your spouse's family. This performance began long before you arrived and it will take you more than a little time to catch up. And by the way, don't let the reviews prejudice your experience of your new extended family members, even if those assessments come from your spouse!

Your spouse's family pageant (whether it is comedy or drama or both) could be viewed as a mystery which has the potential to be great fun as you track down clues to how your in-laws see the world and bring their gifts to bear on it. Certainly your spouse carries traits that have their origin in his or her family and it won't take long to see the family's influence on your partner's behavior. It is also true that your spouse might *not* act like people in his or her family, perhaps partly because of things he or she didn't like growing up. It is important for you to recognize this as well.

Remember, your spouse (and your spouse's family) is also getting to know you and possibly, if you live in close proximity, your folks. Sometimes it is like the Hatfields meeting the McCoys. Other times it is like the gang from *Modern Family*. So give everyone a chance to adjust. Most extended families come to some kind of a working relationship, even if they still consider the other side a "little weird." What is important is that you and your spouse come to an agreement on how you are going to include—and if necessary at times, exclude—your families of origin from your new nuclear family. As you do so, however, keep these things in mind.

- Your in-laws are a wonderful source of information about and support for your spouse. Next to you they may well know your partner better than anyone else. Parents, siblings (and their spouses), aunts, uncles, and cousins can be a rich source of facts, stories, and insights into your new spouse. Listen carefully and you might understand the reason for some of your husband's (or wife's) attitudes and behaviors. And if your spouse is in trouble for any reason, his or her family is often a better source of help for you than even your own family.

- Your in-laws have their own stories to tell. Your marriage is one in a long line of marriages going back generations on both sides of your two families. Think of your own parents standing behind you with their hands on your shoulder, behind them another set of parents for both your mother and father. These are your grandparents, who may or may not be alive, but their stories are part of the legacy of your new family. As you get older, and especially if your marriage is blessed with children, you will wish to know more about the people on both sides who have shaped your family's traditions, beliefs, and view of the world.

■ These family-of-origin stories carry lessons about life and distinguish your family from every other. Family stories help us to stay in touch with what we Catholics call "the communion of saints," that is all those living and dead who have shared in God's boundless love. The stories told in families—your own and your spouse's—will assist you both (and eventually your children) in appreciating the incredibly rich history of your "tribe's" journey.

So look for opportunities to interact with your in-laws. Invite them to your home for a meal, maybe one couple or family at a time instead of the entire clan at once. This is a way to show your new relatives that you wish to have an adult-to-adult relationship. They are your guests in your home, and a meal provides an opportunity for you to engage them in stories about their lives growing up and their experiences as newly married couples themselves.

The stories told in families will assist you both (and eventually your children) in appreciating the incredibly rich history of your "tribe's" journey.

Be prepared to assist your families of origin if needed. One newly married couple we know lives with the wife's parents, and the new couple has made a conscious effort to help with household tasks, contribute financially, and interact with the parents as equal adults. Their presence in the home says to the parents and other in-laws: "We are here for you as an adult couple, just as you are here for us."

Finally, and this is really important, respect the religious traditions of your in-laws, even if you do not follow them or even understand them. You may not agree with their beliefs or the way those beliefs are expressed but, trust us, criticizing or belittling your new relatives' religious beliefs is inappropriate, offensive, unnecessary, and will ultimately backfire on the two of you. Instead, look for the basic values that underlie the particular religious practices of your in-laws and seek whatever common ground you might have with them. For example, buy a book of interfaith or interdenominational prayers that you can use at family gatherings that would not offend anyone who is there and read a prayer before meals or opening gifts at holidays or graduations or birthdays. That is what major religious leaders try to do when they gather for ecumenical or interfaith events.

If you share the same or a similar faith with your in-laws, this could be a rich way to share what you have in common. Attend religious services with them. Ask them to pray for you and promise to keep them in your prayers. If your faiths or practices are very different, talk to them about what it is about your faith experience that gives you comfort. Express real interest in their beliefs, just as you would about anything else that was important to them. You do not have to agree with them in order to exhibit respect. It is a great opportunity to test out what you believe and how you want to handle faith in your own marriage.

Look for the basic values that underlie the particular religious practices of your in-laws and seek whatever common ground you might have with them.

THIRD CHALLENGE

Developing an intimate and faithful marriage in a consumer culture is difficult.

Intimacy in marriage is the closeness and bonding that goes on between the two of you. Fidelity is your commitment to make your marriage remain the #1 thing in your life. Both intimacy and fidelity build across a lifetime together. They increase as the years go by and you build up your unique reservoir of memories, jokes, tender moments, and crises that create the fabric of every long-term marriage. But while they are a major goal of your relationship, intimacy and fidelity are not easy to develop, and a number of things in our consumer-oriented culture can get in the way.

For example, jobs can be a roadblock to fidelity. The contemporary workplace is often one where people work closely together on projects that may last several months at a time. Sometimes it even involves travel together.

Your co-workers may know more about that part of your life than your spouse does. You all speak the same lingo, know about the setbacks and triumphs that happen each day, and share the culture of your workplace that sometimes extends even beyond the hours spent doing the work.

One young woman we know had a boss who would take her and the others in the department out for a glass of wine at the end of the day. Another woman had a boss who expected her to answer his emails even when she was at home in the evening. Both of these situations are an indication of a work relationship that had spilled over into family time and could turn into a threat to a faithful marriage.

For some people it's not work that takes them away from their intimate time with their spouse. It may be other pastimes or commitments. If you have a very consuming hobby, for example, it can eat away at your couple time. We know a young man who is a talented artist. That's not what pays the bills, though, at least right now, so he has to do his painting on his own time. Sometimes that's okay with his wife, but since they've had a baby, it's harder on her. They now have work time, child care time, painting time, and less and less couple time. Not a good formula for marital success.

Our current technological time-absorbers create a challenge for intimacy too. How many times a day do you check your email? Go on Facebook? Surf the web or cable channels for the latest on sports or politics? One newly married couple established rules for the use of the cell phone. It wasn't allowed until after breakfast and during dinner or whenever they were on a "date." They say that saved their marriage in its early years. The easy access to the world through all the electronic devices we own makes it harder to focus on our partner, hard to make space in our brain for the one-to-one sharing that is the bedrock of intimacy.

Even friends can be an obstacle to time alone together. Researchers call the current generation a "Civic" generation, meaning that they like to do things in groups. They have a communal sense and have often spent much of their time before marriage doing most things with a number of friends. It's so easy to arrange to gather by e-mail, texts, e-vites, and events posted on Facebook. You don't have to plan ahead or send paper invitations through the mail—or even call people on a phone—in order to have a gathering. Last minute brunches or parties can happen through the click of a few buttons. All this can be at the expense of the old-fashioned breakfast in bed or curling up alone with your spouse to watch TV or read a book, not to mention making love with each other.

Consider the following suggestions for dealing with these challenges to having the kind of intimate and faithful marriage you're hoping for.

- Make time for each other. Obvious, but serious. Build it in to your rituals and your schedules. Some couples

Make time for each other. Build it in to your rituals and your schedules.

set their morning alarm a few minutes early so they can talk about their day before rolling out of bed. Some have a glass of wine before dinner or a cup of tea together before bedtime. One couple told us they lie in bed every night and share about the best thing and worst thing in their day. Whatever works for you, make it something you do habitually.

■ You may not always be together—again, business trips, emergency visits to family, or military deployments can separate you. Use email or texting or skyping to stay in regular touch while you are apart. A military couple shared that they developed an intimacy emailing each other when he was in Iraq that they missed when he returned. They found that they could be open in their email exchanges in a way that was harder to achieve amidst the distractions in their daily lives.

■ Recognize that sexual infidelity is usually the final infidelity in a marriage, not the first. If you discover yourself flirting with a co-worker or spending time with someone other than your spouse, it's time to do a gut check before it's too late. You may even need to see a counselor, either alone or together, to sort out why you are "falling out of love" with your spouse and come up with a plan to restore the intimacy that is the basis for fidelity in all marriages.

■ The scriptures tell us about the power of a name. "Don't be afraid, I've redeemed you. I've called your name. You're mine" (Isaiah 43:2). Have a pet name for each other that signifies that your beloved is special to you. A name that is just used by you for your love is a sign of the intimacy you share. Maybe you already do, but if not try one and see how your partner responds.

■ Know one or two things that make your spouse feel special and/or sexy. Is it a scented candle burning in the bedroom? Is it favorite music playing when you get home from work or when the kids are at Grandma's? We know a husband who knows what it means when his wife brings home a box of gingersnaps. Like the commercial says: Price, $1.39; putting your husband in the mood? Priceless!

THIRD OPPORTUNITY

Discovering that intimacy and fidelity have a spiritual dimension.

Intimacy, strengthened by fidelity, is the goal of marriage. All the marital skills you read about in self-help books, all the insights present in marital relationship-building classes are designed in one way or another to foster intimacy (and therefore fidelity) in marriage.

In the Catholic tradition, this is one of the two things marriage is all about. It is called the "unitive" dimension of marriage. The other is called the "creative" or "fruitful" dimension. Both reflect the relationship of God to creation and Christ to the church. This is why marriage is a sacrament in Catholicism. In the process of growing in your love for one another you are also growing closer to God: "No one has seen God, ever. But if we love one another, God dwells deeply within us, and God's love becomes complete in us—perfect love!" (1 John 4:12).

Clearly intimacy and fidelity are about more than sex, although they certainly include sexual intimacy, which is perhaps the height of physical and spiritual intimacy in marriage. It also includes a peck on the cheek on the way out the door and a genuine delight in seeing each other again at the end of a busy day.

Closeness is often considered a synonym for intimacy, but it is not the same thing. You can be close to people without being intimate with them at all. Intimacy involves being open and vulnerable in the presence of another. It involves

It is often only within the shelter of a civil and sacramental union that couples experience the trust needed for true intimacy and fidelity.

risk, because if you are rejected by your spouse the hurt can be immense. That's why it's not uncommon for couples to enter into a deeper form of intimacy after the commitment of marriage than they experienced before the wedding. Even while living together before marriage, many couples refrain from fully revealing their deepest selves for fear of rejection. That is not surprising, because the public and lifelong commitment to the relationship has not yet been made. It is often only within the shelter of a sacramental union that couples experience the trust needed for true intimacy and fidelity.

Intimacy also involves empathy, that is, the ability to experience another's joy and pain and to enter into a deep understanding of the meaning and purpose of his or her life.

Marriage provides a unique opportunity for you to be empathetic with another human being.

Recently a family we know experienced the death of a wife and mother. As the family stood at the grave after the burial ceremony, the husband came forward and thanked his wife for all the wonderful years they had together. He praised her for her role as a partner, parent, and grandparent. His three adult children, all with their own spouses at their sides, also came forward to praise and thank their mother. A priest, who was the only other person present, spoke later of the impression this family made on him and how beautifully they supported one another. There was a profound sense of grief that everyone in that family experienced that also revealed a spiritual sense of intimacy.

Marriage offers you many opportunities you may not be able to get anywhere else.

- **The opportunity to know yourself more deeply.** Sharing at this level gives you a chance to reflect on your own hopes, dreams, joys, and sorrows and to find the words to convey them. It also provides an opportunity to receive feedback from someone you know has your best interest at heart.

- **The opportunity to confide in another knowing that you will be accepted as you are.** For many couples, marriage gives them their first experience of unconditional love. Your spouse is not naïve, he or she knows your faults. It's just that your partner sees you through the eyes of love and accepts you as you really are.

■ **The opportunity to grow as a couple.** Intimacy and fidelity builds over time as you experience events as a couple. The first years together establish a pattern to your life: everything from getting up and out to work in the morning to eating together at the end of your day. Small rituals establish a foundation for you as a couple and allow for the unity of your marriage.

Years ago a mother approached us to say that her son and his wife, married less than three years, were getting a divorce. "They were never a couple," she said. "They each had their own friends and their own way of doing things but never seemed to come together as a real unit." Don't let that couple be you. You have the opportunity to make intimacy and fidelity the hallmark of your marriage. Take that opportunity.

 **You have the opportunity to make intimacy and fidelity the hallmark of your marriage.**

FOURTH CHALLENGE

Dealing with religion in marriage requires respect, sensitivity...and compromise.

Being newly married is a formidable thing. You have made a choice that you hope is the last one you're ever going to make in that category. You've linked up with the person you assume is going to be your romantic partner for the rest of your life. As this shift in perspective takes place, however, you may begin to encounter the differences in your core religious belief systems. If that doesn't open the door to some big questions, it's hard to imagine what would!

Before the wedding, you may have glossed over some of these differences about how you view God, the ultimate meaning of life, the source of good and evil, the reason for pain and suffering, what happens after you die, the nature of your vocation, even what you want any potential children to be taught. Families on both sides might have backed off pushing their traditional beliefs and practices in order to keep the "peace." But now that you are newly married, these issues may be taking on more urgency and creating more tension. The two of you may well have had discussions and come to an understanding about issues surrounding the religious education of your children, but developing a family religious tradition and sharing a spirituality with your spouse is a task even beyond that.

A few years ago our niece was engaged to be married to someone from a different faith tradition. She wanted to raise their children in the Catholic faith and, in the beginning of their engagement, her fiancé agreed. As the wedding got closer, however, he changed his mind. Having children practice a faith he was not part of was not something he could accept. Our niece broke off the engagement because they couldn't compromise on this issue. We told our niece it was good he had raised his objections before they actually were married and it was also good that she was clear about how important her religion was to her. She's now dating a Catholic fellow and we hope it works out between them. Even if it does, though, she may be surprised to find that they will still have to work on differences in their approach to Catholic beliefs and spiritual practices.

As we always like to say, all marriages—even those between two Catholics—are interfaith marriages.

If you are both Catholic, were you raised in similar types of Catholicism? The practice of the faith among Mexicans differs from the way the Irish worship, for example. A person whose parents were charismatic Catholics might not understand the practices of someone whose family was a more social activist or pro-life kind. You may have gone exclusively to Catholic schools all your life while your Catholic spouse attended a vacation Bible school at an Evangelical Protestant church every summer. So even if you don't fit the traditional

All marriages—even those between two Catholics—are interfaith marriages.

definition of an interfaith couple, you very well may have the challenges of one.

Being in a committed, lifelong relationship is a way of either doubling or halving yourself. On the one hand, you are not as free as you were when you were single. You now have someone else to consider in almost every decision you make. You are not as able to take any job anywhere, or to stay out all night if you feel like it, or to spend however much you want on your hobbies or interests. On the other hand, you now have someone to help you make decisions and carry them out. If you both have jobs, you might have extra financial resources as well. If you're a glass-half-full kind of person, you see the benefits of having another person to share with. Glass-half-empty types will see the limitations. This works in the spiritual realm as well. When you are married, you cannot practice your faith however you want. You have to take your partner's beliefs, feelings, and practices into account. See what we mean: half-full, half-empty?

Coming together as a couple around life's ultimate questions will involve respect, sensitivity, and compromise, as well as a lot of conversation between the two of you. Here are some suggestions for handling the challenges.

■ Have a formal conversation, perhaps over a quiet dinner, about the way you were raised in terms of religion and what you would hope for in your marriage. Things like "our family always went to church together, and I'd like to get back to going regularly, preferably with you" or "I like the way your family celebrates holidays with Scripture readings at the dinner table" might open up an incredible conversation. Talking about your religious history and the things you see in one another's traditions can help you carve out a practice that is worth trying for the two of you.

■ Think of ways that you can expand shared spirituality into your life aside from attending worship services. Doing some sort of service work or joining a young couples' discussion group or attending a Bible study class together might be of interest to both of you. Your spiritual growth doesn't have to happen just within the walls of a church, synagogue, temple, or mosque.

Your spiritual growth doesn't have to happen just within the walls of a church, synagogue, temple, or mosque.

- If your spouse is not from the same faith tradition as you and offers to come to religious services with you, make sure to help him or her feel comfortable by explaining what is going on. Kneeling, sitting, standing, and other routines can be confusing for those who aren't familiar with the traditions in your denomination. And if he or she comes to your services, be sure that you reciprocate. Or you may be the one who goes first. If so, be gracious and attentive.

- Share prayers at home. There are tons of books available that contain prayers that cut across all religious traditions. You can even find blessings or poems or readings that will be comfortable for someone who professes no specific belief. Some good times to pray together are at meal time, just asking God's blessing on your food; at bed time, talking about what you are grateful for in your day, or first thing in the morning, asking God's help for both of you in the day ahead.

- If either of you is from a tradition other than Christian, there may be cultural issues as well. An article that appeared in *Gourmet* magazine a few years ago highlighted the difference in food traditions in some religions. Hindus, Muslims, and Jews all may have very specific ideas about what can be eaten and in what combinations. It is fun to experience and honor these traditions, especially if they are important to your spouse.

Studies of interfaith couples highlight the fact that when couples work hard to understand their partner's faith and find areas of agreement, religious differences actually strengthen their marriage. So if you are able to find places of common belief and practice in your marriage, whether you are a true interfaith couple or just a couple of Catholics with different experiences, it will repay your effort a hundredfold.

When couples work hard to understand their partner's faith and find areas of agreement, religious differences actually strengthen their marriage.

FOURTH OPPORTUNITY

Sharing a spiritual life is one of the best paths to deeper intimacy.

Dealing as a couple with the inevitable joy and pain life sends you will create a depth of connection that can only be hinted at in the beginning of your marriage. These are the Big Questions that can only be answered on a spiritual level, and it is one of the true joys of marriage to forge a united approach to them. Ask almost any happily married couple.

Within the Catholic spiritual tradition there is a way to live in contemporary society with integrity and purpose, and that is to hold one's own beliefs without being intolerant of others. We Catholics as a group have many particular beliefs and practices that tend to identify us: weekly church attendance, the seven sacraments, devotions to Mary and the saints, beliefs about social justice and the sacredness of life from beginning to end, and many others as well. These are important to us and we have an obligation to live them out in our daily lives. They don't make us better than others or superior to others, but they do hold us accountable to witness our faith and to live in peace and love with those who don't necessarily share all our beliefs.

Marriage provides an opportunity to live in that peace and love with another person in a most special way. Because of the lifelong commitment that is made and the nature of the physical love between the spouses, marriage offers a unique opportunity to share things on a very deep level with another human being. If one of those things can be both partners' spiritual lives, even if they do not share all their religious beliefs and practices, the level of intimacy that can be achieved is astounding. It can become a model for living with integrity, an alternative to individualism, and an antidote to relativism and consumerism.

It's important for us married couples to acknowledge that we have a stake in the larger community beyond our immediate family. Marriage provides the opportunity to move from independence to interdependence. Marriage demonstrates that as adults we are capable of taking care of all our needs independently but choose to relinquish some of our independence for a shared future. We realize something may be lost in this exchange, but much more is gained. All spiritual traditions point to the benefits of healthy sacrifice offered out of love for another. In marriage this circle of sacrificial love grows to include extended families, children and grandchildren, and the larger community.

Another powerful way to support each other and to build a sense of partnership is to pray for your spouse. Many times in the course of your life together, the only thing you will be able to do is pray. Your partner may be going through a crisis such as the death of a parent or sibling. He or she might be struggling with a personal problem or being required to make a difficult decision. You may not be able to lift your spouse's burden, but you will be able to support him or her in prayer.

Here is what married couples know that can lead to their own deeper spiritual intimacy and to a better world for all.

■ Married couples know it is possible to willingly give up some of what we have so that others might have a better life.

- Married couples know that the things we own are not simply our individual possessions but rather a gift entrusted to us for the good of others.

- Married couples know the problems of the world are complex and daunting but can be overcome with hard work, love, and commitment.

- Married couples know we need others to help make decisions and carry them out.

- Married couples know the value of relationship-building—with each other, with extended families, with others in their communities and workplaces, and with God.

Few people have had a direct mystical experience of God, but most married couples have the opportunity to see God's love and experience God's forgiveness through their spouse. When that happens we become a sign for others. That is our vocation as a married couple.

Most married couples have the opportunity to see God's love and experience God's forgiveness through their spouse.

FIFTH CHALLENGE

Ignoring financial situations and differences is a sure path to trouble.

We were talking with a woman whose daughter had gotten married recently, and she told us a story we found shocking. Her son-in-law had purchased a dog for $900 without consulting his new wife. The young man wasn't even working currently. He was in school, trying to establish a new career. The daughter had told her mother, not complaining about her husband's actions so much as worrying about the ongoing cost of food, grooming, and healthcare for the dog. We, on the other hand, saw the problem as much broader, involving how the couple dealt with money and the way they were approaching it.

We suggested to the mother a tool we have used often with young couples to help them sort out their differing attitudes toward finances. It seemed to us that the new husband did not understand that he was no longer a financial free agent and was now in a combined household with a responsibility to make shared decisions about shared resources. And the new wife, well, we felt that she had better learn to speak up—and fast—or this couple was heading down a pretty slippery slope, at the bottom of which we have found a lot of wrecked marriages.

Much like religious differences, almost all new marriages also undertake the challenge of merging two different ways of thinking about, handling, and spending money. As an engaged couple, even if you lived together before the marriage, you may have kept your money separate and felt that you did not have to consult each other about the way you used your own money.

But now that you are married, you are probably revisiting that arrangement, at least to some extent. If you are both working, for example, you are most likely jointly contributing to the household expenses. You may be keeping the rest of your money separate, however, and as such may still feel that you should be able to spend your money as you please. If that's okay with your spouse, then it's okay—period. It's not up to your parents or anyone else to question how money is handled in your new household.

What is important, however, is that you both agree on how you are going handle your money and expenses, both jointly and independently. Pretty much any system can work as long as both partners completely buy in to the system.

That being said, some systems are riskier than others. For instance, we met a woman who told us her father's system was to max out his credit cards and then go on a game show and make enough to pay them off. It had worked for him, but she was not about to plan her marital finances based on his example.

Getting on the same page around your finances is a big challenge, and so is setting mutually agreed upon goals. Do you want to own a house? Do you hope to be starting a family? If you already have children, do you want to plan for their education? Do you want to travel? Do you want to start your own business? Your financial decisions will need to be tailored to your goals as a couple and as a family.

Some of the difficulties in making those joint decisions reside back in your separate families of origin. How was money handled there? We all receive messages about money as we are growing up, and often internalize them. We either play them out in our own lives or rebel against them. What we cannot do is get them out of our heads: "A penny saved is a penny earned," for example, or "Live for today, because tomorrow you may die!" Becoming aware of those messages is the first step of getting control over them and deciding if they work for you in your current situation. Then you have to find out how they fit in with the messages in your *partner's* head.

Another aspect of finances is debt—the debt you bring into the marriage and the debt you incur as a couple. If you have college loans or credit card debt, it's important to be up front about those things with your spouse. Sometimes a husband or wife feels ashamed about the way he or she handled finances in the past and doesn't want to share that "dirty laundry." But finances can only be addressed, and new goals set, if you put everything out on the table. And after the wedding and honeymoon (which you may have borrowed some money to pay for), it can be very tempting (especially if you have two incomes and even more so if you don't realize the extent of your existing debt) to buy a lot of things you "need" now and pay for them with "easy monthly payments."

Who handles the money is another marital challenge. Sometimes no one takes charge, and this can be a disaster. Other times one person agrees to do the finances but doesn't follow through, and this too can cause serious problems. So, you can do it together or name one of you to be responsible, but it needs to be done, no getting around it!

While one of you may be a better money handler than the other, it does not mean all financial issues should be left in that person's hands. It is helpful for both of you to know what's going on with all family funds, including pensions, investments, insurance, and taxes. If anything should happen to the one who handles the money, the other will need to be aware of where things stand. Many a spouse has been hit with the injury or illness or death of a spouse and didn't have the slightest idea how to sort things out. (Speaking of insurance, when you are young is the most advantageous time to buy it, so get yourself a good insurance agent you can trust and talk about what insurance you need and can afford.).

While one of you may be a better money handler than the other, it does not mean all financial issues should be left in that person's hands.

The following are some ways you might use to approach your finances.

- Listen respectfully to your spouse when you are discussing finances. For many of us, talking about money raises our anxiety, so it may be a hard conversation to have peacefully. Some couples have found that it's easier to stay pleasant if they have the conversation in public, out for a cup of coffee, for example. It is also helpful, especially if there are financial problems, to get a trusted financial advisor to talk with you together. It can be a friend or family member you both like and admire, or an outside person whom you pay but has no vested interest in your decisions, but the main thing to remember is that it is still *your* money and *your* financial decisions that are being discussed.

- Be clear about the money rules in your relationship. Is there a limit to how much you can spend without consulting your spouse? Does each of you get a little "mad money" each month that you can spend however you want? What about presents, for each other and for others? Is there a limit on how much you spend on them? What about furniture and groceries and eating out together? You might want to put these decisions in writing, even make it into a formal budget, so there is no misunderstanding or "forgetting" what you decided and you can identify potential problems early and have an objective way to talk about them.

- Establish your financial goals and work toward them. Whether the goal involves *undoing,* something like paying down a debt or loan, or *doing* something, like purchasing a house or taking a vacation, having goals really helps curb impulse spending. Again, talk about them, write them down, refer to them regularly.

■ If you find yourself in financial distress, don't panic. First talk with each other and assure each other that you are committed to resolving the problem. Consult someone you know and trust or a not-for-profit counseling agency. There is good advice out there, including many sources that are based in various faiths and denominations, and you are bound to feel better when you talk over your situation with a person who shares your values and has the knowledge and resources to help you.

■ Finally, put some money aside for others. Whether it's to lend to a needy friend, knowing you probably will not get it back, or contributing to church or charities, make giving to others part of your normal way of handling finances.

If you do these things, you will avoid one of the biggest pitfalls of marriage.

Make giving to others part of your normal way of handling finances.

FIFTH OPPORTUNITY

Living a life of fruitfulness and generosity is what marriage is all about.

There's an old saying that you've probably heard: "Two can live as cheaply as one." The theory is that once you are married you will need just one household, one trip in the car will get the two of you where you want to go, one heating bill warms the two of you, and cooking for two is almost as cheap as cooking for one. While you may have found out already that the math isn't quite that simple, it is true that being married does reduce some of your expenses, even if it doesn't cut them in half.

Here is the real opportunity, however. Not only can you save on some of your expenses as a married couple, but if you want to you can discover the spiritual joy and satisfaction of having your relationship bear fruit and overflow beyond just the two of you. Of course, having children is one of the hallmarks of marriage, but kids are not the only way that couples can be fruitful and generous.

Here are some of the opportunities being married presents to increasing and sharing what you had as individuals.

- You will learn other ways to handle money. It is very likely that your partner does not have the exact same approach to money that you do. You have developed a way of handling money since you were on your own. Maybe it works well for you, and maybe there are some ways that you could be doing a better job.

It's possible that the things that are difficult for you financially are the very ones your spouse does well. A woman we know was bad at keeping records of her spending. She was not in debt, but where her money went was a mystery to her. Sometimes she had money left over at the end of a pay period, and other times she was scrimping to make it to her next paycheck. She married someone who was a very good record keeper. He set up a simple computer program where she could enter her expenditures daily. It was not meant to be a judgment on how she used money, but just a way for her to see where it went. Suddenly, she could make her financial decisions based on real knowledge, and it helped both her and her husband be more frugal and therefore have more to share.

- You will have someone you trust to discuss finances with. We live in a culture that gives contradictory messages about money to us. We are told we should save for our retirement (even when we are quite young), that we should put money away for college (even if we do not yet have children), or should save for a down payment on a house. But then we are bombarded with ads encouraging us to spend our money *now*. We're even told that the national economy suffers when people aren't spending! So how do you sort out these messages and make a responsible pattern for yourself? Having a person you love, who has agreed to share your life from here on, is a comfort and an opportunity to pick a path based on the best knowledge and experience of both of you.

■ You don't have to do it all at once. You are together for the rest of your lives (we hope and pray). You don't have to be the perfect money managers today or tomorrow. What a consoling thought that you have all the time in the world to become the fruitful and generous couple you hope to become. If you decide you spent too much money on eating out one month, try to eat out once less the next month. If you bought too many clothes last year, buy one or two fewer outfits this year. One couple we know loved to buy art, but when they got married their available wall space

You have all the time in the world to become the fruitful and generous couple you hope to become.

quickly filled up, so they made a deal with each other that they would only buy a piece of art that both of them loved. It saved them a lot of money, but it also made them more discriminating art buyers. You get the picture (pun intended): Go slowly, and congratulate each other for each step you make toward your financial goals.

Go slowly, and congratulate each other for each step you make toward your financial goals.

■ Your shared values will help frame your decision. One of the ways most couples line up well in pre-marital personality profiles is over their values. It's rare when the two don't say they have similar values, and we're pretty sure it was true of you. Now that you're married, however, your spending habits can reflect those values in a very real, concrete way. It's easier to spend less on hobbies when your spouse reminds you that you both agreed to support the disaster relief fund this month. Or you can delight your spouse when you suggest that it would be great to give his or her younger brother money toward college. You can decide that it is okay to take that lower paying job with a not-for-profit organization when you know you have the loving support of your spouse.

■ Generosity is good for marriage, and marriage is good for generosity. Recent studies indicate that generosity is a key element in a strong marriage. This is not just talking about money but also the spirit of giving freely without looking for payback. Marriages that have a high degree of generosity indicate a high degree of happiness on the part of both spouses. Making charitable giving part of your budget is a way to extend the love you have for each other to the entire world.

AFTERWORD

We hope that this little booklet has helped you see that marriage is going to provide you with challenges and opportunities enough to fill your days. Like us, you'll be able to say that your life is never boring and can be filled with love.

Please keep in mind these words of St. Paul:

Agree with each other, love each other, be deep-spirited friends. Don't push your way to the front; don't sweet-talk your way to the top. Put yourself aside, and help others get ahead. Don't be obsessed with getting your own advantage. Forget yourselves long enough to lend a helping hand.

Philippians 2:2-4

Remember that marriage works if you work at it, and focusing on each other is the way to true intimacy and ultimate happiness for a married couple. There is nothing in the world more desirable and satisfying than these two things.

God bless you both.
Kathy and Steve Beirne

RESOURCES

If you have enjoyed reading *Catholic and Newly Married* and found it helpful, please consider subscribing to *Foundations Newsletter*. Information is available at foundationsnewsletter.net or call 207-775-4757.

- *Beginning Your Marriage* by John L. Thomas, S.J. Chicago, ACTA Publications, 2002, 800-397-2282, www.actapublications.com

- *For Better, For Worse, For God* by Mary Jo Pedersen. Chicago Loyola Press 2008, 800-621-1008, www.loyolapress.com

- Money Habitudes by Sybil Solomon, Wilmington, NC, Life Wise/Money Habitudes, 888-833-4331, www.moneyhabitudes.com

- *The Power of Commitment* by Scott Stanley, San Francisco, Jossey Bass Publishers, 2005, 800-956-7739, www.josseybass.com

- www.foryourmarriage.org. This website is really a door to many resources on marriage and especially Catholic marriage. You will find stories, articles, video clips, book reviews, interviews, and links to local resources.

ABOUT THE AUTHORS

Kathy and Steve Beirne have extensive experience in Catholic marriage and family education, catechetics, and marriage ministry. They are the editors and publishers of the *Foundations Newsletter for Married Couples*, which has gone out to over 100,000 newlywed couples over its years of publication. They have written many magazine articles, served as advisors to the bishops' committee on Marriage and Family, and spoken widely on topics relating to marriage. The Beirnes have recently developed a conversational tool for couples called FACET, which is included in ACTA Publication's marriage preparation workbook, *Perspectives on Marriage*.

Kathy has an M.A. in Child and Family Development from the University of Missouri. Steve has an M.A. in Catechetical Theology from Manhattan College. The Beirnes live with their extended family in Maine.

OTHER BOOKS FOR COUPLES

Perspectives on Marriage. Full of down-to-earth activities and practical advice on everything from finances to communication to spirituality to intimacy. Double copies of each exercise provided for easy sharing. 80-page workbook

Beginning Your Marriage. An insightful, comprehensive presentation of the important issues and critical life skills that contribute to a successful marriage. 158-page paperback

Prayers for the Newly Married. Forty reflections and prayers that address issues such as daily married life, sexual love, families and friends, children, and key anniversaries. 95-page hardcover gift book

Daily Meditations (with Scripture) for Busy Parents. Inspiration, wisdom, insight, and joy for every day of the year for parents of children of all ages. 252-page paperback

Available from booksellers or call 800-397-2282
www.actapublications.com